I0439958

San Luis Obispo

Freemasonry

1860 - 2013

PETER CHAMPION

Copyright © 2012 Peter George Champion

www.MasonicTrivia.com

All rights reserved.

ISBN-13: 978-1481023986
ISBN-10: 1481023985

:

DEDICATION

To the future generations of Freemasons
who will share Masonic ritual, spiritual growth,
fraternal fellowship, philanthropy, and family fun
within the beauty of the temple on Marsh Street.

CONTENTS

Acknowledgments   i

Masonic Abbreviations &   iii
   Appellations

1 Introduction - 1913   1

2 San Luis Obispo Lodge No. 148   4

3 King David's Lodge No. 209 - 1870 8

4 King David's Lodge No. 209 - 1913 14

5 The Architect   32

6 The Contractor   37

7 The Masters and Early Leaders   39

8 The Modernization and   58
   The Restoration

9 The Festivities   65

10 The Charity and The Future   71

About the Author   73

ACKNOWLEDGMENTS

Kudos: To the nineteenth century brethren of King David's Lodge who had the vision of future generations of Masons in the city of San Luis Obispo, California. To the brethren of the twentieth century who built the temple on Marsh Street. To the twenty-first century brethren who were stewards of the historical integrity of the Temple while upgrading safety features and modern conveniences. To all the Lodge Officers who prepared, stored, and preserved King David's Lodge minutes and Tiler's registries, architect's plans, and photographs.

As with any book, the author's job is akin to herding cats during a thunderstorm. Each item of fact gleaned from research sends the author scrambling to all points of the compass. This book would not have been possible without the support of my local Masonic brothers, the Grand Lodge of California, local newspapers, the San Luis Obispo Historical Society, and the descendants of John Davis Hatch and William John Smith.

Special thanks to my wife of forty-three years, Jan, for proofreading draft after draft; to twice Past Master M. Robert Bettencourt, Esq. for bringing historical material to light; to Lodge Secretary George Brown III for raising early Lodge photographs from a filing cabinet and closet grave, and to District Inspector and Past Master David Chesebro for historical suggestions and awesome editorial skills.

PETER CHAMPION

MASONIC ABBREVIATIONS & APPELLATIONS

Bro.   **Brother** (name)

The term may reference a fellow member of a particular Lodge or a member of Freemasonry in general.

Master   *The current or then current presiding officer of the referenced Lodge*

PM   (name) **Past Master**

A former presiding officer of any Lodge

W. Bro.   **Worshipful Brother** (name)

Either a Master or Past Master of any Lodge.

Worshipful is an honorific more commonly used in England; as in, "the Right Worshipful Lord Mayor of Oxford Charles Smith."

Honorable is the honorific more commonly used in the United States; as in, "the Honorable Mayor of San Luis Obispo Cate Smith."

INTRODUCTION

THE CITY OF SAN LUIS OBISPO

MARSH STREET

MARCH 14, 1913

Friday, March 14th, 1913, was a sunny day in San Luis Obispo, California, with little wind to kick up dust from the shoes of children running in the dirt of Marsh Street.

School boys in tapered wool Knickerbockers, Norfolk jackets, and brown leather high-top Buster Brown shoes were probably glad to be out of school and romped in the street as their parents' attentions were focused elsewhere.

Fashion conscious ladies wore the popular *Tailleur* style high-waisted jackets reminiscent of the *Directoire* style clothing of the 1830s. Some of the full length skirts were trimmed short enough to give a glance of ankles in high heeled boots, a post-Edwardian trend seen lately on Cromwell Road, Kensington and Chelsea, London. All the ladies wore extravagantly massive-brimmed, feathered hats from milliners and purveyors such as Judkins and McCormick Co., Stern Bros., Aitken, and Phipps.

Most of the men wore the simple derbies in vogue for that day; a few wore wide ribbon fedoras, and fewer still wore cow-

1

boy hats to shield their eyes from the bright central-coast sun. Two lines of Freemasons occupied the east and west sides of the center of Marsh Street. All of the men in line wore white aprons at the waists of their suits.

Between the two rows marched a contingent of Masons wearing the colorful Masonic traveling regalia of the Grand Lodge officers of California. The procession also included the noted San Francisco architect John Davis Hatch.

As Most Worshipful Grand Master John D. Murphey was unable to attend the celebration, his pro-tem, Junior Grand Warden Francis Valentine Keesling walked beneath a squared arch formed by the hooked rods of the two Grand Deacons as the rows of aproned men doffed their hats and sideliners directed their attention to the procession. Why was such a large attendance of people gathered in the heat and dust of the central coast? They'd congregated to participate in and bear witness to the laying of a cornerstone for the new four story temple for King David's Masonic Lodge No. 209, Free and Accepted Masons. Both the city of San Luis Obispo and the local fraternity of Freemasons were in a phase of rapid growth.

The Marsh Street building would not be King David's first temple, nor was the name "King David's" the first choice of its brethren. This Temple would be the brethren's fourth meeting house since King David's was chartered in 1870 and the third cornerstone laid by the brethren for their Temples. King David's wasn't even the first Masonic Lodge in the city. San Luis Obispo had been the site of fervent partisanship during the Civil War and a briefly lived Masonic Lodge.

This elegant new Temple building was to be framed of wood with massive redwood support beams, and reinforced with concrete. It was engineered by a famed Masonic architect to be impervious to the likes of natural disasters, such as the recent 1906 earthquake in San Francisco, a mere two hundred and twenty-five miles to the north of San Luis Obispo. The aesthetic furnishings and fixtures were custom crafted by local and foreign artisans for both "strength and ornament". Those 1913 Masons, standing in the Marsh Street dust, built their Temple to withstand the ravages of the coming century. It is now our turn to celebrate the centennial of this great Temple.

San Luis Obispo, Marsh Street, March 14, 1913

SAN LUIS OBISPO LODGE NO. 148

Freemasonry in the city of San Luis Obispo began a decade before King David's Lodge No. 209 was formed.

The power of granting Masonic Dispensation to form a Lodge is confided in the person of the Grand Master of each jurisdiction. The Grand Lodge of California was formed in 1850. A mere decade later, Freemasonry came to San Luis Obispo.

Upon the recommendation of Mineral King Lodge No. 128 in Visalia, the petition to form a Lodge in San Luis Obispo was received by Grand Lodge on September 25, 1860. On September 26, 1860, the Most Worshipful Grand Master N. Greene Curtis of the Grand Lodge of California granted a dispensation to the brethren petitioners of San Luis Obispo to form a Lodge. The actual Charter for San Luis Obispo Lodge No. 148 was granted on May 16th of the following year at the Twelfth Annual Communication of the Grand Lodge of California.

THE FIRST OFFICERS OF
SAN LUIS OBISPO LODGE NO. 148

Worshipful Master	Dr. Joseph M. Havens PM
Senior Warden	Thompson D. Sackett
Junior Warden	Abraham Blochman
Treasurer	Moses Cerf
Secretary	Walter Murray
Senior Deacon	John McElrath
Junior Deacon	Joseph Lee
Tiler	James White

Political division and free state versus slave state issues in the county fostered by the ongoing Civil War and desires to divide California, coupled with the devastating 1863-1864 drought, doomed the longevity of the Lodge. With the loss of livestock and crops, the bulk of the Lodge brothers deserted the region with their families, seeking fertile land and survival. The few remaining brothers caved to reality, and at the Stated Meeting of December 2, 1865, voted with regret to surrender their Charter.

The founding Master, Dr. Havens, was not present for most of the famine years. Being a man of wanderlust, he had moved to Paita, Peru, in the spring of 1863 when he assumed the post of United States Vice-Consul. During his time as Master of the Lodge, he was the county's judge. When Havens moved, W. Bro. Walter Murray assumed his duties as Master through the remainder of the Lodge's existence. (More on the famous Walter Murray comes later on page 53)

The Seal of Lodge No. 148, the Charter, the officers' jewels, the Tiler's registry, and the minutes of the Lodge were all sent to the Grand Lodge in San Francisco. Fate and California's geology intervened and all the materials were destroyed in the Great San Francisco Earthquake and Conflagration of 1906.

During the short term of San Luis Obispo Lodge No. 148, they conferred only one Master Mason degree. If any Lodge were to claim they only Raised one brother during their term, none could do better than San Luis Obispo Lodge No. 148. The brother they raised was José Antonio Romualdo Pacheco, Jr..

Bro. Pacheco was the second native Hispanic-Californian to be raised a Master Mason; his uncle, Julio Carrillo of Temple Lodge No. 14 in Sonoma, was the first to have received the honor. Bro. Pacheco was distinguished within and without the Lodge. Within Masonry, he was the Marshal of San Luis Obispo No. 148 in 1863. He was also became a member of the Royal Arch Masons and a Knight Templar in the Commandery.

Bro. Pacheco was a rancher and a judge who became active in San Luis Obispo and state politics. Unusual by today's standards, he held positions in both the Democratic and Republican parties. In 1863, he married the 22 year old flamboy-

5

ant conversationalist Mary Catherine McIntire. An accomplished playwright and published novelist, her play *Incog* had a long run in both London and New York to critical acclaim. Pacheco financed theatrical productions of her dramatic comedies, *Loyal to Death* and *Nothing But Money*.

Bro. José Antonio Romualdo Pacheco, Jr.

He was elected to the California State Senate, became the ninth State Treasurer in 1863, the ninth Lieutenant Governor in 1871, and the twelfth Governor of California in 1875. He remains the only Hispanic Governor of the State.

In 1877, he was elected to the U.S. House of Representatives and was sworn in as the first Hispanic Representative with full voting privileges. He was re-elected in 1879. After leaving Congress, he moved to Coahuila, Mexico, and raised cattle.

He served a term as Regent of the University of California. He was briefly the Warden of San Quentin Prison. In the 1880s, he co-founded Hale & Pacheco Mining Investments in San Francisco.

In 1890, he was appointed United States Envoy Extraordinary and Minister Plenipotentiary to the Central American States.

He was the first Governor of California to be a native Californian and the only native Californian Governor to have been born before California received statehood.

The 1800s were a dangerous and adventurous time to live in the city and county of San Luis Obispo. As we will read later, many of the hardy Masons in San Luis Obispo braved ruffians, outlaws, brigands, and homicidal desperados. The grit of Bro. Pacheco that allowed him to face the treacherous battlegrounds of politics came from his time on the central coast facing more feral ruffians. Troops of *ursus arctos horribilis* or grizzly bears were so prevalent in early San Luis Obispo that the beast is prominently depicted in the forefront design of the County Seal. As an expert horseman, Bro. Pacheco holds the distinction of being the only governor of any state to have lassoed a grizzly bear from horseback.

KING DAVID'S LODGE # 209

1870

Modern San Luis Obispo Freemasonry is traced to 1870. None of us were alive at the time. So a little fun history, as to events of that year, may put the time into perspective.

Belgian chemistry professor E. J. DeSemdt patented a process for asphalted pavement. As a demonstration to its advantages over gravel or oyster shell, he installed a short strip of roadway in front of the City Hall in Newark, New Jersey.

Construction commenced on the Brooklyn Bridge. New York City opened its first subway line. Transcontinental rail service began.

The Fifteenth Amendment, granting racially free suffrage, was ratified in 1870, "the right of citizens of the United States to vote shall not be denied or abridged by the United States or by any state on account of race, color, or previous condition of servitude."

Rev. Hiram Rhodes Revels, Mississippi, was sworn in as the first black member of the United States Senate. He assumed the chair vacated by Jefferson Davis in 1861.

Joseph Hayne Rainey, South Carolina, was the first black man sworn into the United States House of Representatives.

Suffragist Victoria Claflin Woodhull opened a Wall Street Brokerage Firm. She became the first woman nominated for U.S. President, but could not cast a vote for herself.

Harper's Weekly published a cartoon by Thomas Nast that was the first characterization using a donkey as a symbol to identify the Democratic Party.

The United States began minting silver coins at Carson City, Nevada. The first coin was a Seated Liberty Dollar.

The First Vatican Council dogmatically defined the doctrine of pontifical infallibility, against the dissent of Bishops from Germany, Austria, Switzerland, France, and Hungary.

Virginia, Texas, Mississippi, and Georgia were the last four states readmitted to the Union under the Reconstruction Acts.

SAN LUIS OBISPO

W. Bro. Walter Murray's younger brother, Bro. Alexander Murray, died in May 1870. Alexander was a prominent local citizen and involved in multiple businesses and occupations: Postmaster, County Superintendent of Schools, Wells Fargo agent, Internal Revenue collector, sewing machine salesman, and proprietor of a saloon in San Luis Obispo. Alexander was a member of San Simeon Lodge No. 196 in Cambria until moving to Santa Barbara and affiliating with Santa Barbara Lodge No. 192. Alexander's death, from tuberculosis at only thirty-six, was front page news in the local paper. The fact that Alexander's brother Walter was the owner and editor of the paper might explain the large black border around the front page and the headline, "A Public Calamity". Some wags may have thought the prospect of the Murray "social club" going out of business more the calamity, they had no reason to fear. The paper reported that the establishment had been rented by C. H. Mock, who would reopen the club soon in "elegant style".

Santa Barbara Lodge requested the brethren of San Simeon to conduct Bro. Murray's funeral in San Luis Obispo. What is now less than an hour's drive on a modern highway was an all day trek in 1870 for the men of San Simeon Lodge in Cambria. With no suitable Masonic facility in San Luis Obispo, the proceedings were held at the rented Odd Fellows Hall.

Masons gathered after the funeral at 4 p.m. on May 18, 1870, in the adobe building on Monterey and Chorro used by the Odd Fellows as their hall, and discussed the need for a local Masonic Lodge in the blooming community below Caliente Peak. One week later, thirteen Masons assembled and petitioned the Grand Lodge for a dispensation: James H. Blackburn; William Freeborn; Benjamin Grable; William S. Harriman; Michael Henderson; William Jackson; Irvine Johnson; Simon Krollik; Walter Murray; Bryce Patrick; Levi Rackliffe; James B. Sutherland; and Newton Witt.

The name chosen for the new Lodge was Pratt's Lodge, in honor of the presiding Grand Master of California, Leonidas Pratt. At a subsequent meeting, the Biblical significance of David being anointed King after the death of his friend Jonathan was not lost on the Masons, and the name King David's Lodge was suggested and adopted. King David's Lodge held its first meeting on June 24, 1870, under a dispensation granted by Grand Master Leonidas Pratt only eight days before, and elected officers. The Grand Lodge issued a Charter at their twenty-third Annual Communication on October 14, 1870.

THE FIRST OFFICERS OF KING DAVID'S LODGE

Worshipful Master	Levi Rackliffe PM
Senior Warden	Michael Henderson
Junior Warden	Newton Witt PM
Treasurer	Irvine Johnson
Secretary	Walter Murray PM
Senior Deacon	David Mallagh
Junior Deacon	James Sutherland
Senior Steward	William Freeborn
Junior Steward	William Harriman
Tiler	Simon Krollik

Additional members included: William Jackson PM, James Blackburn, Ernest Cerf, David Ely, Joseph Fisher, Isaac Goldtree, Benjamin Grable, William Hays, Archibald Jesse, Lazare Landeker, Isaac Leby, Henry Loobliner, Bryce Patrick, and Horatio Rembaugh.

Without a building of their own, they rented the meeting hall of Chorro Lodge No. 168 of the International Order of Odd Fellows for every Tuesday, Wednesday, and Friday for the sum of fourteen dollars a month. Dues were set at two dollars per quarter. Twelve men paid $10 apiece to fund the Lodge. It cost $90 for the dispensation petition fee, $1.90 to send the petition to Grand Lodge, and pre-paid return postage of ninety cents. Thus the opening Lodge budget had assets of $27.80, not enough to pay for the first two months of rent.

The first "permanent" two story Temple was constructed in 1874 for $3,511.82. This sum included the plot of land, the building, the furnishings, and the carpet. The construction was funded by subscriptions and a mortgage of sixteen hundred dollars. It was situated on Higuera Street between Chorro and Morro Streets. The ground floor produced rental income from two mercantile tenants. This temple served King David's well until outgrown in 1894. In 1894, there were 44 states in the Union, one automobile in the US, Coca Cola first sold in bottles, and the membership in King David's had surged with the increase of numerous brothers from the Southern Pacific Railroad and the influx of businesses to the city and county. In addition, the concordant bodies of San Luis Chapter No. 62 of Royal Arch Masons, warranted April 11, 1883, and San Luis Obispo Commandery No. 27 of Knights Templar, warranted April 29, 1887, occupied the same limited facility.

The first order of business at the first stated meeting in the new Temple was passed by a narrow vote of eight in favor and six against. The resolution read, "To pay a fine of 50 cents for any person who spits upon the carpet." The six votes in opposition bode of the clash that plagued the brothers for years to come over how the Lodge was to be managed. The formation of the Masonic Hall Association on March 18, 1889, and its assumption of the financial affairs of the lodge quelled some of the hot-blooded dissention among the brethren.

The second "permanent" Temple was built and dedicated on St. John the Baptist's Day of June 24, 1894. It was located on the corner of Chorro and Marsh Streets. Lodge assets had improved from the original $27. The new Temple cost $10,489.52. The Junior Grand Warden William Thomas Lucas, of Santa Maria, officiated at the dedication ceremony. The first degree conferral in the new building was on Louis Felix Sinsheimer. (A short biography appears on page 48)

The 1894 Lodge Room offered a spacious floor area for ritual and drill team practice by the Sir Knights of San Luis Obispo Commandery No. 27

The Commandery is commonly referred to as the Christian branch of Freemasonry or Knights Templar. The Order is noted for the large ostrich plumed chapeaux, swords, baldrics, and military uniforms worn by its Sir Knights.

Seven Masons under the leadership of Dr. William William Hays, gathered in the doctor's office on March 27th, 1886 for the purpose of forming a Commandery in San Luis Obispo. Ventura Commandery No. 18 endorsed the petition for a dispensation. The dispensation was granted to San Luis Obispo Commandery No. 27 on June 14, 1886. Ventura Commandery loaned the fledgling group necessary regalia, furniture, and paraphernalia. By the following April, the membership had more than quadrupled, and the Sir Knights had raised the funds to furnish a complete set of furniture, regalia, and paraphernalia. The Grand Commander of the State of California, Reuben Lloyd, issued the warrant for the Commandery on April 29, 1887. In the first four years, the Commandery grew to forty-eight active members. During the San Luis Obispo Commandery's history, Sir Knights displayed their military drill in numerous local and state parades (see page 66 photograph). Several of Commandery No. 27's early Sir Knights formed an equestrian team (see page 46 photograph).

A dispensation was granted on November 14, 1882, to form a chapter of Royal Arch Masons in San Luis Obispo. Grand High Priest William Petrie issued the warrant establishing San Luis Chapter No. 62 on April 11,1883, to Levi Rackliffe. More about the remarkable Bro. Rackliffe can be found on page 40.

The dispensation to form a local Council of Cryptic and Select Masons was granted on October 4, 1926. Grand Illustrious Master William Duggan issued the warrant for San Luis Obispo Council No. 38 on April 18, 1927.

While all three bodies have memberships that include companions and Sir Knights from throughout the local Masonic District and the California Central Coast, they have always held their monthly Stated Meetings in King David's Temple buildings and have been instrumental in financing each new Temple erected In San Luis Obispo.

KING DAVID'S LODGE

1913

Let's start with some historical background for 1913.

The Sixteenth Amendment to the Constitution was ratified, giving Congress the authority to levy an income tax without apportioning it among the states.

The first word ever filled in a crossword puzzle was the preprinted word, F-U-N. Arthur Wynne invented a diamond shaped puzzle in the *New York World* for the December 21, 1913, edition of the paper. In 1914, he pioneered the use of blacked out squares in his puzzles and his past-time game spread "across and down" the country.

Ebbets Field opened in Flatbush as the home stadium of the Brooklyn Dodgers, but without blue rally monkeys.

William Merriam Burton patented a thermal cracking system that doubled the yield of gasoline from each barrel of petroleum. Henry Ford's adaptation of assembly lines to the automobile industry assembled a vehicle from the pre-fabricated parts to a completed car in under three hours. From Times Square in New York City to Lincoln Park in San Francisco, The first transcontinental trip on the Lincoln Highway took thirty-four days. Only half of the road was "improved" with gravel or oyster shell.

Eight years after immigrating to the United States from Sweden, electrical engineer Otto Fredrik Gideon Sundback patented the zipper, which revolutionized galoshes (clothing came later). Mary Phelps Jacob invented and patented the modern brassiere, giving a lift to women's fashion.

Harry Brearley, an English metallographer, developed a means of protecting rifling in gun barrels. He initially called his new alloy, that added chromium to steel, "rustless steel". He changed the name when a local cutlery manufacturer came up with "stainless steel".

Oregon enacted the nation's first Minimum Wage law. South Africa banned blacks from ownership of land. The First Balkan War ended. The Second Balkan War began.

Two years after having been stolen in France, the *Mona Lisa* was recovered in Italy. R. J. Reynolds introduced a blend of Virginian and Turkish tobacco in packaged cigarettes under the brand name of *Camel* cigarettes.

Capt. Pyotr Nikolayevick Nesterov of the Imperial Russian Air Service performed the first aerobatic loop of an airplane. Engineers claimed the maneuver, "impossible".

Future President Richard M. Nixon was born. Gerald Ford, who would assume the presidency when Nixon resigned, was born.

The United States Post Office began Parcel Post delivery service.

THE 1913 CORNERSTONE

The opening chapter of this book set the scene in Marsh Street on March 14, 1913, as Freemasons, family, and onlookers gathered for the laying of the cornerstone for the new Masonic Temple. Forty-three brethren and officers of King David's Lodge signed the Tiler's Registry. Fifty-five visitors signed the registry. The visitors were mostly from California, but included Masons from Canada, Texas, Oregon, Washington, Michigan, New York, Iowa, and Minnesota.

Among the visitors was the architect who designed the new temple at the request of the Hall Association and Lodge. Their wisdom in the selection of John Davis Hatch as the architect is revealed in the next chapter.

Officiating at the cornerstone ceremony were Junior Grand Warden Francis Valentine Keesling and the Worshipful Master of King David's, P. H. Murphy.

Francis Valentine Keesling

W. Bro. Keesling was an attorney in San Jose. His father was from Indiana and his mother was a native of Mexico. In 1910, he ran for Lt. Governor of California on the Republican ticket. In 1914, he ran for Governor. Keesling was a Major in the National Guard and served with distinction during the great fires that followed the San Francisco earthquake of 1906. He was the 1916 Grand Master of Freemasons in California.

He was well known to and popular with the men of King David's Lodge. Keesling was active in the York Rite, Scottish Rite, and Shrine. He was an avid golfer. His socialite wife, Haidee Grau, was the hostess of lavish parties and the darling of the San Francisco press society pages.

County Auditor P. H. Murphy,
1913 Master of King David's Lodge

There is a misconception that the symbolic cornerstones of buildings are of structural importance. But, symbolic cornerstones are infrequently included as part of the structural foundation. They are usually placed above ground where visitors and passers-by can read the inscription with ease. There is a common practice in making the symbolic cornerstone hollow and placing a sealed casket inside containing mementos related to the building and the time of construction. The cornerstone symbolically laid on March 14, 1913, held such a casket. Its contents included:

- *List of officers and members of King David's Lodge No. 209 F.& A.M.*
- *List of officers and members of San Luis Chapter No. 62, R.A.M.*

- *List of officers and members of San Luis Obispo Commandery No. 27. K. T.*
- *List of officers and members Corona Chapter No. 107, Order Easter Star with postage stamp attached including one parcel post and two 1915 Exposition stamps.*
- *An autograph list of the City, County, and Federal officials.*
- *An autograph list of Masonic Hall Assn. Directors, Architect, and General Contractor.*
- *Bottle of corn, bottle of wine and bottle of oil.*
- *Copy of the March Trestle Board.*
- *Copy of the Tribune*
- *Copy of the Telegram*
- *One five cent, ten cent, twenty-five cent, and fifty cent piece, all 1913 coinage.*
- *Copy of the serving program in honor of the Grand Lodge officers and laying of the corner stone.*
- *Historical sketch and list of Past Commanders and officers and members of San Luis Obispo Commandery No 27, Knights Templar compiled by Sir Knight John H. Hollister.*

On the Friday of the laying of the cornerstone, the brethren gathered in the existing Masonic Temple and the Grand Lodge of California was opened in Ample Form. Grand Lodge was called from labor to refreshment for the purpose of laying the cornerstone, and the men adjourned to Marsh Street for the ceremony. Afterward, Grand Lodge was closed. King David's minutes reflect, "In the evening, a banquet was served in honor of the visiting Grand Officers and brethren."

An anomaly occurred in the laying of the cornerstone. Masonic tradition holds that the cornerstone is the first stone laid, and it is to be laid in the northeast corner of the building. Because of the configuration of King David's Temple with its entrance facing the southwest to northeast running Marsh Street, the cornerstone was symbolically laid in the due north corner of the building, facing the northwest.

*An elevator and driveway now stand on the
ground occupied by the church in this photograph*

March 14, 1913, cornerstone ceremony

Another view of the cornerstone laying ceremony

*March 14, 1913, celebratory banquet
honoring Grand Lodge officers*

The Dedication

Front page news was made by King David's Lodge on December 19, 1913, when the completed Temple was dedicated.

The act of dedicating or consecrating a Temple to a particular service is an ancient practice. References are extant of the dedication of the Temple of Solomon when its building was completed. It was again dedicated in the time of Hezekiah and the Second Temple was dedicated by Zerubbabel, and again after the Syrians were expelled.

Modern Masonic dedication ceremonies began with the publication of the Prestonian Lectures in the seventeen hundreds. William Preston mentions that the ancient Lodges were dedicated to King Solomon. Modern Masonic Lodges are dedicated to the two Holy Saints John: Saint John the Evangelist and Saint John the Baptist. A depiction of both Saints is found in two locations in King David's Lodge. One is to the left of the Worshipful Master in the East and another is next to the door of the elevator in the Assembly Room.

King David wrote in Psalms 104:15-16 that "And wine that maketh glad the heart of man, and oil to make his face to shine, and bread which strengtheneth man's heart. The trees of the Lord are full of sap; the cedars of Lebanon, which he hath planted."

The dedication of December 19, 1913, followed the ancient Masonic practice of pouring corn (bread), wine, and oil on a model representing the completed Temple. This was done in the Lodge Room that bore the same beautiful wallpaper that still adorns the room a century later.

The wallpaper represents the cedars of Lebanon and the oculus in the ceiling permits filtered sunlight light, supplemented by indirect lights around the top of the wallpaper to illuminate the room in an impression of standing among the cedars with the light filtered through the trees.

The cedars wallpaper was prepared on special Martin H. Birge leather printed hangings that gave what E. O. Lynne of the *Tribune* remarked as, "the twilight of departing day casts a mellow and yet cheerful glow."

The Martin H. Birge & Sons (George and Henry, both Harvard graduates) Company of Buffalo, New York, produced premier wallpapers from 1824 to 1976. Beginning in the late 1800s, they were noted for their reproductions of colonial and European wallpapers, including those of Mount Vernon and the elegant Morris Jurmel Mansion that was George Washington's headquarters during the Revolutionary War and where he dined with his Cabinet on July 10, 1790.

For the dedication ceremony, the Lodge Room was set up with extra chairs to accommodate the massive crowd of Masons, their families, guests, dignitaries, and onlookers. The architect's model and elements for the ceremonial ritual were laid out within the room. These preparations made it impossible for the Grand Lodge to open in the Lodge Room, so Junior Grand Warden Francis Valentine Keesling and the Grand Lodge officers retired to the new Library room where Grand Lodge was opened in Ample Form. Several speakers were invited to present informative talks during the dedication. Architect John Davis Hatch addressed the Masonic significance of the new Temple. Acting Grand Marshal (and actual Grand Secretary) John Whicher addressed the history of King David's Lodge. W. Bro. Whicher was an author of Masonic history books and a Past Master of King David's Lodge.

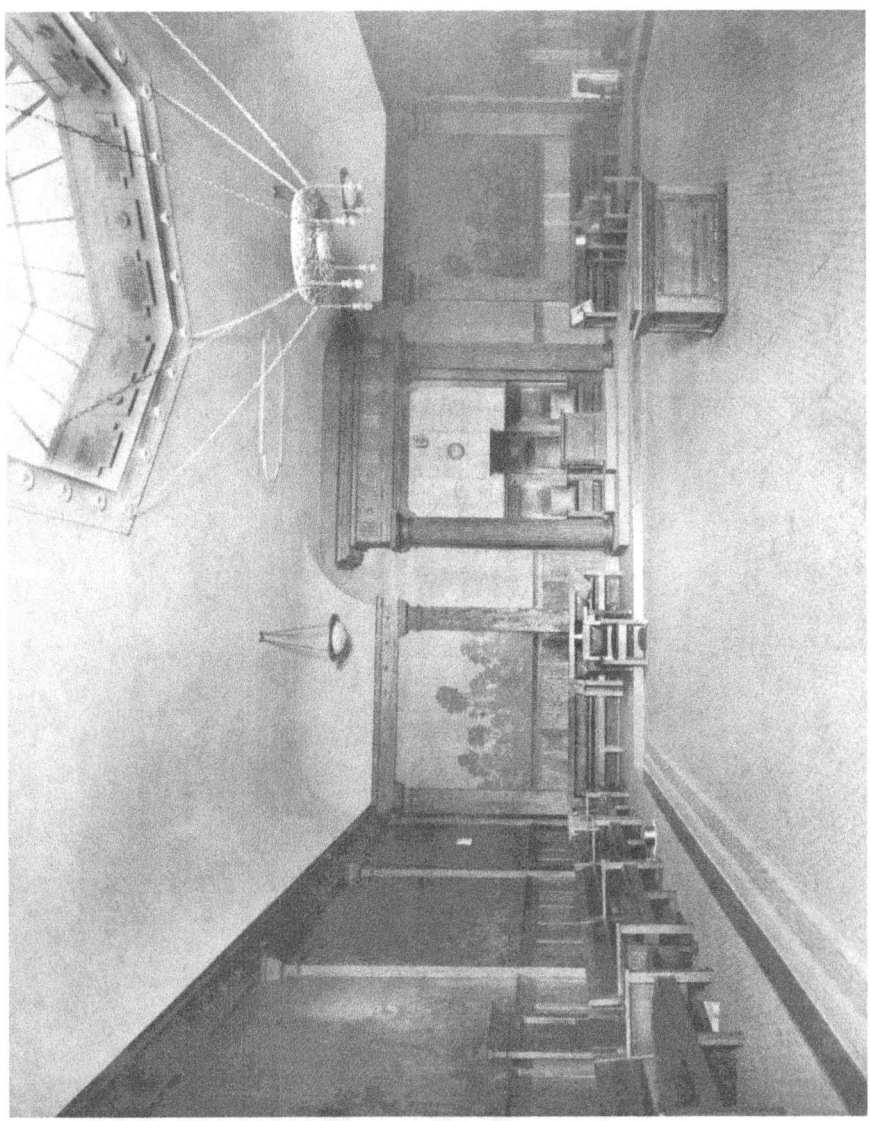

The original six lights dangling from the wreath and the lights around the outer hexagon of the oculus, as seen in this 1913 photograph, were removed in the 1970s. There were originally four carved marble hanging lamps in addition to the indirect lighting behind the entablature or superstructure of moldings atop the pilasters around the room.

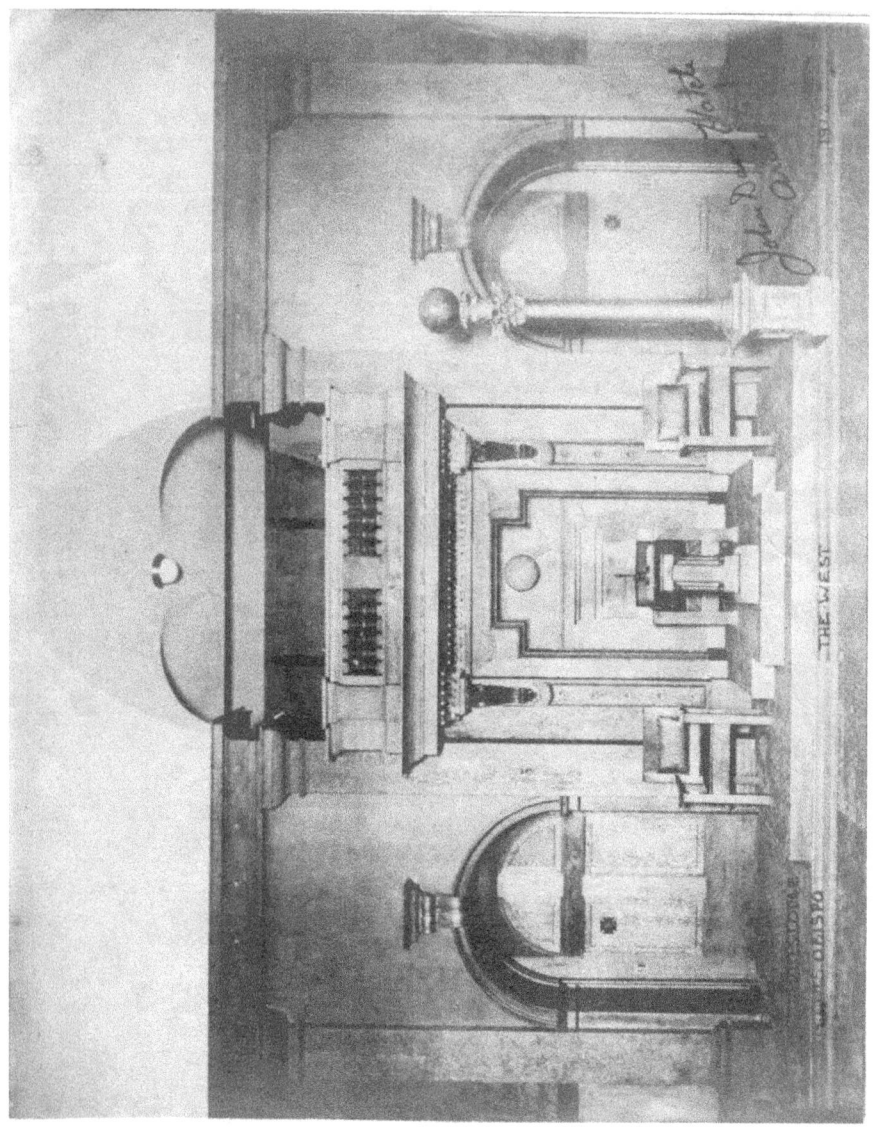

The organ loft above the Senior Warden's chair in the West of the Lodge Room was designed to accommodate a pipe organ. In 1913, it housed a pianola style player piano. This 1913 photograph is signed by the architect, John Davis Hatch.

The Architect's plans labeled the room seen in this 1913 photograph, "the Assembly Room". Over the century, it was alternately called the Smoking Room and Lounging Room. It has contained both a billiard table and a pool table. The hooded fireplace and andirons were said to be of Middle English design. The walls were finished in leather. There was a time in the 1990s and 2000s when it housed a converted coin-operated pocket pool table.

Custom brass and plated fixtures filled the lodge, from door knobs to push plates, all bearing a Masonic Square and Compass theme.

The ground floor contained two rental spaces. The first tenants were the San Luis Furniture Company (responsible for supplying most of the Lodge furniture) on the south and the business offices of the local telephone company on the north of the entrance.

The upper floor held the "Armory" for the Knights Templar to store their swords and uniforms, office space, seven apartments suitable as living quarters, a bath and two showers. Several Masonic brothers worked for the railroad and during their layovers rented the third floor apartments.

The Dining Hall's maple wood floor was covered with a heavy canvas carpet that could be rolled up for ballroom dancing after banquets. The Dining Hall walls were painted in soft tones of meerschaum, tan, and gold.

Among those firms responsible for the Temple's construction were Union Hardware & Plumbing; J.R. O'Mara, heating and radiators; W.V. Fisk, electrical sub-contracting; G.W. Gilbert, interior designing and decorating; D & N.E. Walter of San Francisco; specialty furniture design; Roberts Manufacturing Company of San Francisco, specialty designed electrical fixtures; and W. J. Smith, the general contractor.

The Ladies Parlor was furnished with "Veal Reed" appointments and "Grass Matt" floor coverings. The doorway in the center opens into the Library Room. Originally, a large fireplace was to be in the Library at this spot with enclosed bookcases framing it. Before construction, the fireplace design was moved to the Assembly Room. The white bookcases stayed and are still in the Library.

The maple wood floors of the Lodge Room and the stairwell planks were covered with "the finest Wilton velvet carpet". The sideliner seating was padded leather pews. They can be seen around the walls in this photograph of the Lodge Room set up for a ceremonial of the Knights of Malta in 1914.

This third Temple was the most expensive and most lavish of King David's three sites. The two adjoining lots on which it sits were purchased for $5,000 apiece. The construction of the Temple building, fabrication, and furnishings cost a staggering sum for its day, $57,093.16.

Financing was raised through the sale of shares. There were numerous private and Masonic subscribers throughout the community, including substantial support from the Commandery of Knights Templar and the Order of Eastern Star.

1913 view of King David's Temple from Marsh Street

Over the past century, the two storefronts on the ground floor have been rented to a furniture company, the phone company, a hobby shop, a surfboard and surf clothing store, and a bank. The roof currently has two rentals for cellphone towers. The income from the tenants supports scholarships, Lodge maintenance, Lodge activities, and philanthropies.

THE ARCHITECT

John Davis Hatch

John Davis Hatch, born in Rye, Westchester, New York, in 1875, was the son of another famous architect by the identical name. Like his father, the architect of King David's Lodge designed buildings that are included on various historical registries.

Bro. Hatch became known in California as *"The Architect of Masonic Temples"*. Among the multi-storied California halls he designed are Brooklyn Masonic Temple for Lodge No. 225 in Oakland, the Masonic Temple in Vallejo, the Modesto Temple, and King David's Temple in San Luis Obispo. Among his famous non-Masonic designs is the 1914 Carnegie Building in Ukiah, California.

Bro. Hatch was a graduate of the University of California, Berkeley, and a member of the American Institute of Architects.

Freemason ritual selects tools and implements of architecture as allegories and mnemonics in its ritual, so it is only natural that an architect of Bro. Hatch's caliber would be drawn to the craft.

Bro. Hatch was a member of Brooklyn Masonic Lodge No. 225. He was the architect of their Spanish Colonial Style Temple in August 1910. The two storied building on the southeast corner of Eighth Avenue and Fourteenth Street, Oakland, had store fronts on the ground level. Construction was influenced by the 1906 earthquake. Hatch used reinforced concrete finished with a rough cast pebble dashed cement and heavily beamed ceilings supported with Howe trusses. The interior walls of the building had Doric pilasters, wainscoting, and concealed electric lighting illuminating the soundproof ceiling. There was an assembly area for the Lodge, also known as a "smoking room", furnished with a large open fireplace, and the ladies' parlor was colonial white. All of these features were incorporated three years later in King David's Temple.

Bro. Hatch's connection to San Luis Obispo was more than fraternal, his wife of over fifty years, Gretel, was the daughter of Judge Virgil A. Gregg of the Superior Court of San Luis Obispo. John and Gretel were married June 21, 1904, in San Luis Obispo.

Francis V. Keesling officiated at two cornerstone laying ceremonies for California Masonic Temples designed by Bro. Hatch. The first was at King David's in San Luis Obispo, and the second was four years later on August 11, 1917, for Stanislaus Lodge No. 206. Stanislaus Lodge was a two and a half story building erected at the corner of Fifteenth Street and J Street in Modesto, California.

Bro. John Davis Hatch's signature from King David's Lodge Tiler's Register for the 1913 cornerstone ceremony

Bro. Hatch was present for the dedication of King David's Masonic Temple in 1913, but could not attend the dedication in Modesto in 1917. In 1916, Bro. Hatch "joined the colors" as a volunteer in the Coast Artillery of the National Guard. He was commissioned a 2nd Lieutenant on March 19, 1916. Shortly after the cornerstone ceremony in Modesto, Bro. Hatch had to surrender the overseeing of the work to his associate, William A. Newman, as Lt. Hatch was "called up to the front".

Lt. Hatch served with the American Expeditionary Force, Unit 705 Water Supply Service of the Engineer Department, in Europe. His expertise as an engineer and overseeing a water project in San Francisco was most useful with his duty of providing fresh water for the troops and Medical Department.

Lt. Hatch was President of The Fellowcraft Club for his unit. Under his leadership, the Club provided entertainment for the men and were responsible for the second section of the Third Degree ritual in the Field Military Lodges. During his tour in Europe, money was being raised to erect the Lincoln Memorial in Washington, D.C.. Hatch's name is recorded as President of The Fellowcraft Club in the roster of military groups who donated funds for construction of the Memorial.

Page 35 shows the original 1913 plan for the front elevation of King David's Temple as laid down by architect John Davis Hatch on vellum.

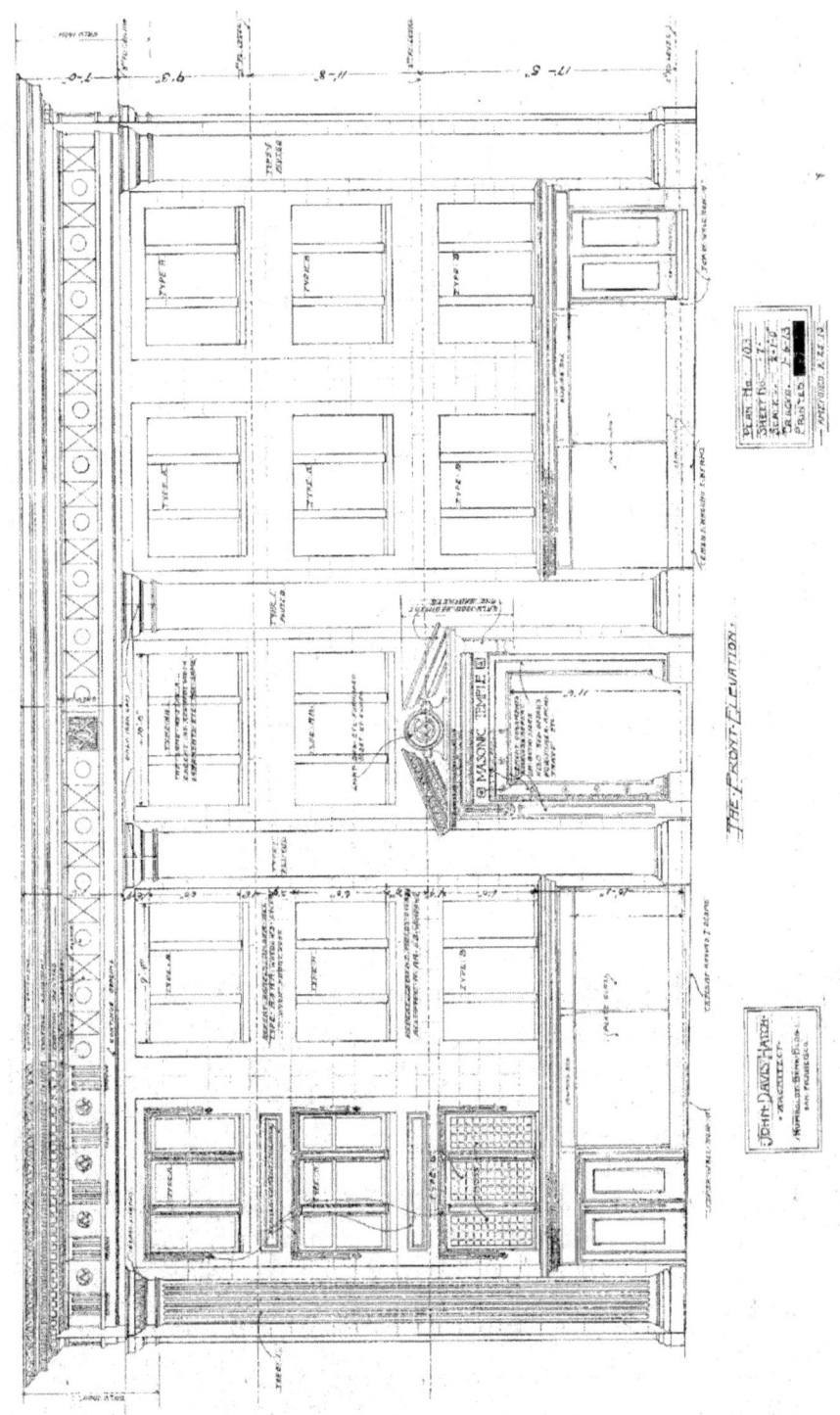

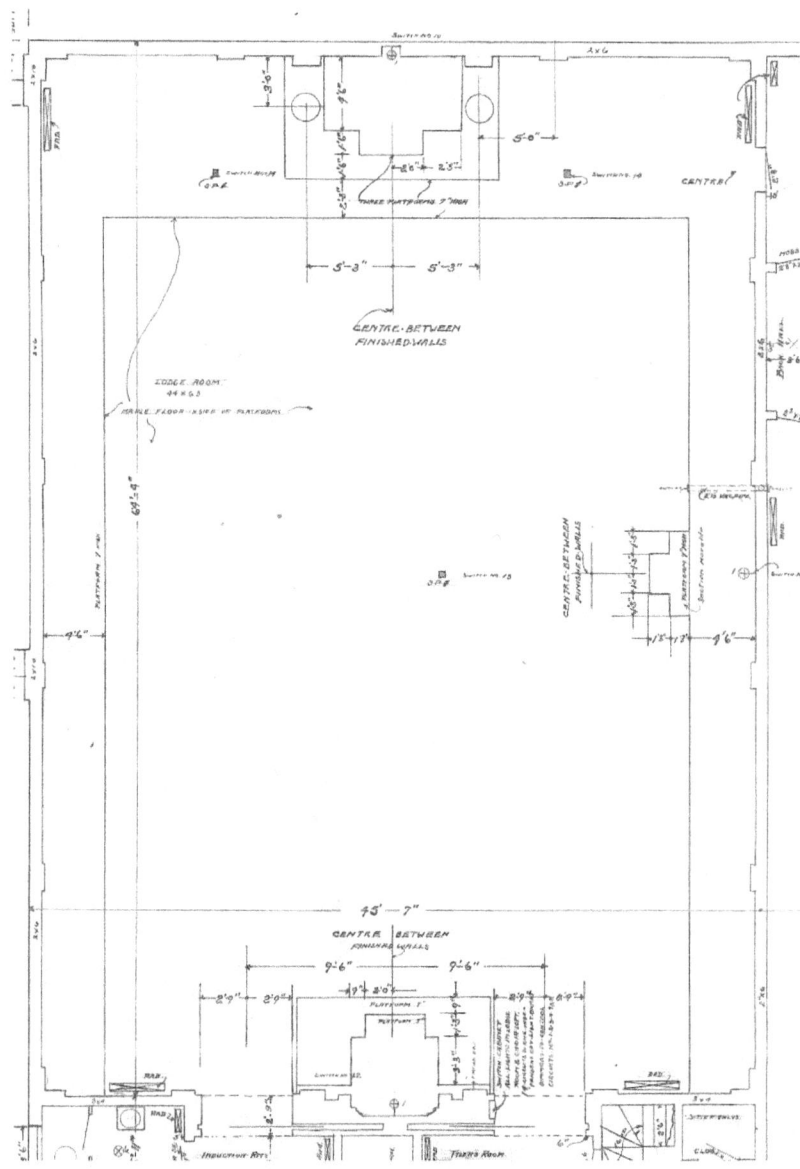

Depicted is the original 1913 plan for the Lodge Room. Bro. Hatch's note in the upper left of the plan reads, "LODGE ROOM, 44 x 63, MAPLE FLOOR INSIDE OF PLATFORMS". The platform around the North, East, and South walls was a rise of seven inches and 4' 6" wide on the North and South sides.

THE CONTRACTOR

The contractor and builder who executed the plans laid down by architect Hatch was Bro. William John Smith.

A native of Pennsylvania, Bro. Smith was thirty-two when he and his wife Harriet arrived in San Luis Obispo County in 1890.

The photograph of Bro. Smith on the left shows him at the apex of a line of Sir Knights gathered for an Easter Observance in front of the Temple he erected. (see page 65 for full photo)

Soon after Smith's arrival, he was conducting his contracting business out of his home in Arroyo Grande. One of his first major projects was in a government project. In 1891, he constructed the first public school in Arroyo Grande. The school had been designed by a local pastor, Rev. W. B. Bell. While in Arroyo Grande, Smith joined Arroyo Lodge No. 274. His construction business prospered, and he moved his offices, family, and Masonic affiliation to San Luis Obispo sometime between 1902 and 1906.

Besides Smith's affiliation with King David's Lodge, he was a companion in San Luis Chapter No. 62 of Royal Arch Masons and an Eminent Commander of San Luis Obispo Commandery No. 27 of Knights Templar. In addition to these Masonic organizations, he was active in Elks Lodge No. 322.

Bro. Smith built several structures that are on the "must see" list for historians and architectural buffs visiting the central coast. Among them are the Milpitas Hacienda north of San Simeon and designed by famed architect Julia Morgan for William Randolph Hearst in 1930. Smith constructed the five houses at San Simeon Bay near the beach in 1928 for Hearst's high-level employees that formed the "Little Spanish Village". In addition to building the Milpitas Hacienda and "Little Spanish Village" for Hearst, he oversaw the construction of a warehouse, a bunkhouse, portions of the castle, and the Hearst "Chicken Ranch".

In San Luis Obispo, he built the Sandercock House at 591 Islay Street in 1927; Dr. F. R. Mugler's House at 1460 Mill Street in 1925; the Bradbury Sanitarium at 743 Buchon Street in 1911; and the Louisiana Clayton Dart craftsman bungalow style home in 1912 at 1318 Pacific Street. Not only did Smith build the Dart house, he designed it.

His close collaboration with architect Julia Morgan and publisher William Randolph Hearst at the San Simeon estate spanned many years and lasted until Smith's death on March 21, 1932. Both King David's Lodge and San Luis Obispo Commandery No. 27 advertised in the *Daily Telegram* for public attendance at his funeral. As reported by the paper, his casket was conveyed to King David's and placed in the Lodge Room of the grand building he had constructed. His funeral service was conducted by both the pastor of his Presbyterian church and the brethren of King David's. .

THE MASTERS

AND

EARLY LEADERS

The Masters of King David's Lodge Chronological Order

Levi Rackliffe 1870, 72-78
Michael Henderson 1871
Phillip F. Ready 1879-80,
   1906-07
William W. Hays 1881-84
William H. Spencer 1885-
   86
George B. Staniford 1887-
   90
Fredrick Adolphus Dorn
   1891-92
Benjamin Brooks 1893
Robert Edgar Jack 1894-95
Ralph Parker Sutcliffe 1896
Daniel Marcus Garrison
   1897-98
Harry Ewen McKennon
   1899
Kaufman Green 1900
John Whicher 1901-02
Louis Felix Sinsheimer
   1903-04
Albert Henry Nelson 1905

George Merritt 1906-09
Walter D. Adriance 1910-
   12, 17
P. H. Murphy 1913
John Sherman Bailey 1914
J. Clifton James 1915-16
Oliver H. P Meck 1918
Edward H. Adams 1919
Maurice F. Dyer 1920
Archie V. Cline 1921
Carl L. Schulze 1922
Francis Horatio Troop 1923
Walter L. Ramage 1924
Grant Lee Cramer 1925
Warren G. Overpack 1926
Ruben R. Long 1927
Robert Dowdle Squire 1928
Robert Wiley Frazier 1929
Nathan S. Lewin 1930
Lucien J. Defosset 1931
Elmo E. Burris 1932
Frederick H. Johnson 1933
Lyle Fenton Carpenter 1934

Howard Buckley Kirkland 1935
Carl W. Pate 1936
William Arnel Sharp 1937
Carl Kirkeby 1938
William P. Inman 1939
John W. Coleman 1940
Lornez V. Richardson 1941
Clyde H. Snyder 1942
Bernhardt R. Preuss 1943
Earl S. Wise 1944
Loran T. Curtright 1945
Elmer G. Grove 1946
W. H. Gaskin 1947
Chestine E. Jones 1948
Morris E. Butler 1949
Casper J. Weir, Jr. 1950
Jack R. Gray 1951
David W. Gleason 1952
Kline J. Williams 1953
Gail B. Goddard 1954
W. E. Snowman 1955
Lloyd G. Stone 1956
John Gaustad 1957
Stanley H. Nelson 1958
George R. Wiech 1959, 67
Harry K. Wolf 1960
Howard Stornetta 1961
Richard H. Hoffman 1962
C. Herold Gregory 1963
Howard Franklin 1964
Dan H. Wasson 1965
Harry W. Austin 1966
Stanley E. White 1968
Emet N. Biddles 1969
Charles O. Blodgett 1970
T. E. Baumberger 1971
Lewis G. McCall 1972
Eldon S. Nelson 1973, 98

Carl J. Weaver 1974
Theodore F. Martin 1975
William J. Edwards 1976
Warren E. Clark 1977
Douglas T. Yungling 1978
Cleatus L. Beatty 1979
Earl L. Parker 1980
Emil S. Thompson 1981, 2000
William B. Boone 1982
John H. Hooley 1983
George O. Burr 1984
Allan B. Goldsmith 1985
Corwin M. Johnson 1986
Thomas D. Hawkinson 1987, 92
William E. Long 1988, 2002
Joe W. Dale 1989
Thomas McLaughlin 1990
William S. Howell 1991
William R. Van Houten 1993
Thomas E. Baumberger 1994
Allan B. Goldsmith 1995
Philip J. Maniaci 1996
Ralph T. Temple 1997
Ken W. Fowler 1999, 2001, 04, 07
John C. Myers 2003
Ivan S. Cliff 2005
David L. Chesebro 2006
Ronald L. Ritter 2008-09
M. Robert Bettencourt 2010, 12
Phillip J. Mauk 2011
Peter George Champion 2013

THE FIRST MASTER
LEVI RACKLIFFE

Levi Rackliffe was born circa 1843 in Lincolnville, Maine. In 1862 he was a 2nd Lieutenant, fighting with the 19th Regiment of the Maine Volunteers, Company A. After the Civil War, he sailed west and settled in San Luis Obispo.

A school teacher by trade, W. Bro. Rackliffe was the first Master of King David's Lodge in 1870 Under Dispensation, skipped 1871, and served as Master for the next seven years. He was also the first High Priest of the San Luis Chapter No. 62 of Royal Arch Masons. Prior to arriving in San Luis Obispo, he was the charter Master of Russian River Lodge No. 181, of Windsor in Sonoma County.

He was elected California State Treasurer in 1895 and held the office at the time of his death on April 21, 1898. He is buried in the Sacramento Historic City Cemetery. His son Carl followed in his father's footstep as a Freemason.

MICHAEL M. HENDERSON

W. Bro. Michael Henderson was initiated an Entered Apprentice Mason upon turning twenty-one in Tuolumne County in 1850, making him one of the earliest men to be made a Mason in California. Henderson, a native of Scotland, had come to California as a Forty-Niner in search of gold. He paid his way as the ship's carpenter. Placer mining proved less profitable than expected. Putting his carpentry skills to use, he found work as an architect. With a little legal study in the art of land

development, he discovered a better way to mine a profit from the land. W. Bro. Walter Murray was responsible for bringing the benefits of San Luis Obispo to Henderson's attention. In San Luis Obispo, he was the Chief Superintendent of Construction on the County Courthouse and was responsible for much of the structural work used on Saint Stephen's Episcopal Church. For many years, he was a local Justice of the Peace.

Henderson was a charter member of San Luis Lodge No. 148. Later, he was the first Tiler of San Simeon Lodge No. 196. In May 1870, Henderson was elected Secretary of the newly formed I.O.O.F. in San Luis Obispo.

Later the same year, he was the first elected Master of King David's Lodge No. 209 under Charter.

In 1871, the 41 year old bachelor married 27 year old local beauty Adela Delisequez, whose father had come to California from France. The next year, Michael and Adela had a son, Alexander James Henderson. Tragedy struck two and a half years later when their boy died of fever.

Adela's death in 1895 left Henderson heartbroken. She was buried in the local cemetery on land that Henderson had donated to King David's Lodge in 1874. Michael followed her in death seven years later. In 1970, King David's Lodge dedicated a stone in the cemetery to him.

Frederick Adolphus Dorn

One of the most distinctive landmarks in San Luis Obispo is the Dorn pyramid mausoleum in the Odd Fellows Cemetery.

W. Bro. Fred Dorn was a native Californian, born in Marysville in August of 1865. He graduated from Hastings College of Law a month shy of his twenty-first birthday. On March 30, 1887, he was Raised a Master Mason in Mission Lodge No. 169 by his brother, Marcellus, who was the sitting Master of the Lodge.

Dorn moved to San Luis Obispo in early 1888 and affiliated with King David's Lodge on May 23 of that year. In November of 1890 he married Cora Belle Russell, the "wealthy in her own right" daughter of a prominent San Luis Obispo family.

In 1891 and 1892, Dorn was Master of King David's. He was active in York Rite, the Odd Fellows, and the Native Sons of the Golden West. In 1894, he was elected District Attorney of San Luis Obispo County, but his major source of wealth came from property investments and inheritance.

The couple was childless when they moved to San Francisco in 1904. Tragedy struck the Dorn family in May 1905. Fred Jr. was born on the twenty-third of May and died the same day. His mother followed him three days later.

Grief stricken, Dorn purchased property in the San Luis Cemetery on a high knoll that had a strong supporting base of olive-green serpentine rock.

Stonemasons hand hewed granite blocks for the imposing twenty-seven foot tall pyramid. The stones were quarried near Porterville, California, and transported one-hundred eighty miles to the cemetery on specially designed wagons. The mausoleum cost over $75,000 by the time it was completed in 1906. This was at a time when a typical five-room house could be purchased for $1,250. Carved within the stone are three names, along with their dates of birth and death: Cora Russell Dorn, Fred Adolphus Dorn Jr, and Fred Adolphus Dorn. Space was left to enter the father's date of death at a time when he would join his wife and child behind the deep green patina of the copper door to the tomb, and the final three ashlars would be mortared into place. But, that day never came. Dorn married Zoe Grey Wilkin of New Zealand in 1908. They had three sons before Dorn's death in 1940. He was buried in San Mateo in a family plot.

JOHN WHICHER

W. Bro. John Whicher was born on the Fourth of July of 1855 in Urbana, Ohio, to Isaac and Rachel Whicher. When he was two, the family moved to Iowa. When the Civil War erupted, his father and brothers volunteered, leaving young John as the only child at home with his mother. John apprenticed to a printer at the age of thirteen. After graduating from public school, he attended Keokuk Business College. While in Iowa, Whicher joined Pioneer Lodge No. 22. John was the only surviving child of eight children. In 1879, he was in Leadville, Colorado, but found mining not to his liking and returned to printing. Whicher became a charter member of Leadville Lodge No. 51 when it formed in 1882. It was the same year he married Isabelle Hoffman of Iowa. In 1886, he moved to Los Angeles, but was wooed away with an offer by the editor of the *Tribune*.

Whicher moved to San Luis Obispo in 1887 to follow his trade in printing at Murray's newspaper, the *Tribune*. In 1894 and 1898, he was elected County Clerk. Beginning in 1899, he also managed the County Bank of San Luis Obispo.

He was Master of King David's Lodge in 1901 and 1902, and served terms as High Priest of the San Luis Chapter of Royal Arch Masons and Eminent Commander of the San Luis Obispo Commandery of Knights Templar. He was the first Exalted Ruler of the San Luis Obispo Elks. He moved to the state capital in 1903 when he was appointed Deputy Superintendent of State Printing.

W. Bro. Whicher served as Grand Secretary for the Grand Lodge of California from 1908 through 1940, a period of 32 years. He was the author of several books on Masonic history and gave the nation's first radio broadcast of a lecture on Freemasonry on September 3, 1921, from San Francisco.

Captain James Cass

James Cass was born in Bristol, England, on November 24, 1824. His first voyage at sea was when he was eleven. He started the voyage as a passenger, but was part of the crew as a "Ship's Boy" by the time the vessel made land in New York. After several years of Hudson River trade and voyages to the West Indies that nearly cost him his life, he returned to England and attended the Elm Academy in Brockley, London.

He shipped out for California gold country aboard the "Orpheus" in 1849. Arriving in San Francisco on July 8, he was engaged as a river pilot the next day at $150 a month. He tried a hand at mining on Amador Creek, but winter mining was not in his blood. He opened a dry goods store, sold it; purchased a farm, sold the farm; bought another store, sold the store; returned to mining; took up farming; got married to Mary Stone; sold out his farm; and took up a government claim on 320 acres in Cayucos. He sold this ranch and put up a combination warehouse and house. With each sale, he turned a profit.

It was in 1872 that he began building the famous wharf and a church in Cayucos. In 1875, he purchased three blocks of waterfront property and built a warehouse. His wharf could handle the traffic of steamers hauling beef, cheese, hides, and apples out to northern ports. More importantly, they brought in lumber to be sold at Cass's profitable lumberyard.

Bro. Cass was active in the Masonic Lodge, but was noted for his enthusiasm in the Knights Templar activities and the Shrine. He held all chairs possible in the Elks and was a member of the Cayucos school board.

DIONIGI "DENNIS" FILIPPONI

Bro. Filipponi came to California from Ticino, Switzerland, in 1869 by way of the Isthmus of Panama. By the time he arrived in California, he was without funds. He took work at a sawmill in Sonoma until obtaining a position at a Marin county dairy. He was a charter member of the Dairyman's Union of San Francisco and was its Director for several years. During

this time, he invested his income into stock of the Bank of Switzerland in San Francisco, a very profitable investment. In 1873, he rented a dairy in San Luis Obispo and by 1889 had saved sufficient funds that he was able to purchase his own ranch and dairy. He built numerous improvements on the ranch, including a cheese and

butter house. By 1901, he had expanded his holdings to 895 acres. He owned and operated the Los Osos Copper Mine.

Bro. Filipponi raised Durham and Holstein cows, draft horses, and farmed lima beans and barley. Eugenia Gaggioni was four years Dennis' senior when they married in 1884 in San Luis Obispo. They had nine children. Dennis served as the Superintendent of the Los Osos school and organized the first Library.

Filipponi was extremely active in all aspects of Masonic life as a member of King David's Lodge, the Commandery, and the Royal Arch Chapter. Beside his involvement in Masonry, education, and his church, Filipponi was a member of the Marin County and San Luis Obispo County Republican Central Committees and active in supporting political candidates.

STEPHEN DAVIS BALLOU

Soldier, sheriff, lighthouse keeper, farmer, Knight Templar, and relative of President Garfield; all of these titles applied to Stephen Ballou. He was born in 1845 in Middleport,

New York, in Niagara County. He was only sixteen when he volunteered with the 49th New York Infantry. He fought at Bull Run, South Mountain, Antietam, Fredericksburg, Washington, Petersburg, Yorktown, Malvern Hill, Cold Harbor, Lee's Mills, and Chancellorsville. He was fortunate to have been wounded only twice; once in the leg at Lee's Mills; and in the face at Malvern Hill. After mustering out in 1865, he headed west by way of Panama and settled into prospecting and mining in the mountain rivers of Nevada. Like most prospectors, a second occupation was necessary to survive, and he ended up doing a stint with the U.S. Geological Survey.

In 1868, he passed through San Luis Obispo on his way to Monterey, where he farmed for six years. He took time out from farming to marry Miss Mary Marshall of Santa Cruz. He opened two general stores on the coast; one in San Luis Obispo and another in Lompoc. He sold these and moved to Arizona where he operated another store before moving to the San Joaquin Valley and opening yet another store while simultaneously farming in Fresno County. From Fresno, he returned to San Luis Obispo and operated the Port Hartford Lighthouse in Avila Beach before being elected Sheriff.

He was a member of the Fred Steele Post of the Grand Army of the Republic. In 1904 and 1905, he was the Eminent Commander of San Luis Obispo Commandery No. 27.

WALTER DOUGHTY ADRIANCE

For many years, W. Bro Adriance was the President of the Masonic Hall Association. When the Marsh Street Temple was built in 1913, he was the first Building Manager and lived in one of the seven apartments on the third floor.

The years of World War I were a busy time for W. Bro. Adriance. In 1917, he was in charge of soliciting funds for the new federal building on Marsh and Morro.

In 1918, he was the Eminent Commander of the San Luis Obispo Commander, the Inspector for the 52nd Masonic District in San Luis Obispo, and a member of the Grand Lodge Committee on Returns. In 1919, he was still the District Inspector and on the Grand Lodge Committee on Maintenance of Masonic Homes.

When not attending to Grand Lodge and Knights Templar affairs, he was a merchant of shoes on Marsh Street.

LOUIS FELIX SINSHEIMER

Louis was born February 23, 1859, in New York City to Aron and Jeanette Shinsheimer. Aron was a soldier during the Civil War with the 120th Regiment of the Ohio Volunteers.

In 1886, Aron and family joined his two older half-brothers, Bernhard and Henry, in San Luis Obispo. Henry had been an agent for Koshland Wool Merchants in San Francisco and a leader in the local German Jewish community. They operated a successful dry goods store and were active in vast land developments. In 1894, Aron and his brothers built a San Luis Obispo landmark, a two-story brick and cast-iron façade store designed by local architects Veitch and Knowles.

Louis' uncles preferred a cosmopolitan setting and returned to San Francisco. The Semi-Weekly *Breeze* of March 18, 1898, published a front page feature article about new Letters of Incorporation for the Sinsheimer business naming Aron and his son Louis as the sole owners of the store. It was in this store that Louis developed the skills of negotiating with the various local cultures of settlers: Chinese, Dutch, English, German, Native American, Mexican, Portuguese, and Spanish.

These skills served him well from 1919 through 1939, when he was San Luis Obispo's longest serving Mayor. A notable event during his mayoral tenure included rendering emergency aid during the Honda Point naval disaster in 1923.

In both 1903 and 1904, Louis Sinsheimer was the Worshipful Master of King David's Lodge.

Sinsheimer Elementary School on Augusta Street was dedicated in 1954 and is named for the former Mayor.

After their parents died, W. Bro. Sinsheimer and his sister Gertrude lived in their family home. During World War II, they were active with the local Red Cross and continued in this service until their deaths. Louis Sinsheimer passed away on July 14, 1951, and was buried in the Jewish section of the Odd Fellows Cemetery with his sisters and parents.

ROBERT EDGAR JACK

Robert Edgar Jack was the son of a seafaring father in a long line of seafarers. He was born in September of 1841 near the Kennebec River in west-central Maine. He graduated from the Wesleyan Seminary. During the Civil War, he was with the 56th New York Infantry and saw action during the Draft Riots in New York and at the Battle of Gettysburg.

After the war, he accepted a post as Secretary-Accountant with Colonel W.W. Hollister at the San Justo Ranch in San Benito. Together, the men purchased the Cholame Ranch. Jack married Nellie Hollister, the daughter of Joseph H. Hollister.

W. Bro. Jack started a chain of successful banks in the central coast cities of San Luis Obispo, Paso Robles, Lompoc and Santa Maria.

Between the years of 1890 and 1893, Jack was Chairman of the City Trustees for San Luis Obispo.

He purchased Hollister's share of the Cholame Ranch up-on the Colonel's death, whereon it was renamed "Jack's Ranch". Amassing by then both considerable wealth and sizeable land holdings, he increased the size of the ranch to 58,000 acres, thereby creating California's largest wool producing ranch.

In 1894 and 1895, he was Master of King David's Lodge. During his second year as Master, he built a spur line from the railroad at Oceano to the beach and built a Victorian Pavilion to attract tourists. It was an ill-advised investment. But, the Victorian "Jack House" he built in San Luis Obispo is a historical treasure, and is still popular with tourists.

W. Bro. Jack was active in the local Knights Templar Commandery, the Royal Arch, and Republican politics. He was a delegate to the national convention that nominated Benjamin Harrison for the Presidency.

WALTER MURRAY

Walter Murray was short in height, big in stature, and one of the more colorful men in California. It has been said that Murray, more than any other brother, was responsible for the re-birth and growth of Masonry in San Luis Obispo. He filled his forty-eight years on this earthly domain with more adventure than men of twice that longevity can lay claim to.

He was born in Gloucestershire, England, in 1826, to James and Sarah Murray. His parents saw to his education through six schools until he was apprenticed to a London barrister. With a group of legal apprentices, he formed a social guild that collected funds to send two of their members to the United States. Lots were drawn and Elmer Filmer with Murray were the two selected to travel. Murray did not tell his parents of the move, and sailed without a goodbye. He never returned to England nor saw his parents after his trip to Boston in 1842.

His first work in America was not in law, but in printing. After gaining experience as a printer's devil in Boston, he obtained a job with the *New York Sun*.

He volunteered to go to California with Captain John Charles Fremont in 1846 as part of the force organized by President James Polk for the Mexican War. He sailed to California as part of Colonel Jonathan Stevenson's Regiment, with stays in Rio de Janeiro and Santiago before arriving in San Francisco. He saw action against the Mexicans in La Paz from July through December 1847.

The California Gold Rush attracted his attention in 1849. He made his way to Sonora, where he met a widow from Chile,

Mercedes Espinosa Quisieros. They were married in 1853 and at the suggestion of Romualdo Pacheco, the future Governor of California, they moved to San Luis Obispo. Murray built an adobe at the foot of Cuesta Grade where he operated a grist mill when not teaching school, studying law, and assuming his duties as Acting Justice of the Peace.

Murray passed the bar exam in September of 1854. In 1858, he was elected to the California Assembly. In 1859, he was elected County Treasurer. In 1867, he was elected District Attorney. In 1873, he was appointed Judge for the three counties of Ventura, Santa Barbara, and San Luis Obispo.

He founded the local newspaper in 1869, *The Tribune*, and was its chief editor. The four page paper was noted for including a couple of columns of news written in Spanish.

Murray was one of the charter members of San Luis Obispo Lodge in 1860, and was its second Master. He was instrumental in bringing many Freemasons to the area and was a charter officer of King David's Lodge in 1870.

At the time of his arrival, San Luis Obispo was known as *"El Barrio de Tigre"* or "The Town of the Wildcat". It was one of the roughest hinterland burgs west of the Mississippi River.

The lawlessness of 1858 incensed Murray, and he called a meeting at his adobe to organize The San Luis Obispo Committee of Vigilance, complete with a charter and bylaws. This did not sit well with Pio Linares, the leader of the Jack Powers-Linares-Valenzuela Gang of desperados. Linares and his gang shot up Murray's house and threatened to batter their way inside, but the outlaw men showed their cowardly colors and turned yellow before making entry.

A posse of vigilantes with Murray and Daniel Blackburn in the lead pursued the outlaws. Linares had a reputation for murdering witnesses and was considered an especially brutal killer. A two day battle ensued in which Murray was wounded, a vigilante named John Matlock was killed, Linares was killed, and two outlaws were captured. They were later hung.

In 2011, the brethren of King David's Lodge, repaired and rededicated the vandalized cemetery obelisk marking the grave of W. Bro. Murray in the Odd Fellows Cemetery.

DR. WILLIAM WILLIAM HAYS

While attending medical school at Georgetown University in Washington, D.C., William William Hayes worked as a meteorologist at the Smithsonian Institution. When the Civil War erupted, the Maryland born Hays joined the Union forces as an assistant surgeon. In 1862, enmity between the North and South raged, but the passion in Hays' northern heart was for Miss Sarah Susan Parks, a southern lass of Virginia. They were married that year.

During the war, the doctor was assigned duty in San Francisco at the Presidio. At the conclusion of the war, Hays, with his wife and two daughters, moved to San Luis Obispo. Early histories of the city report that Sarah was the first English speaking woman to take up a permanent residence.

With no hospital or surgery at his disposal, Dr. Hays conducted a practice of house calls using his striking team of matched white horses to reach his patients.

The doctor was known to be generous with his professional services. When families could ill afford cash payments, he accepted produce to defray the cost of treatment and pharmaceuticals. Many indigent patients and widows discovered their medical bills for his services cancelled.

In August of 1867, Hays summoned a group of fellow Episcopalians to his adobe home on south Monterey Street, where they formed the first vestry and assigned duties. The following month, Bishop Ingram Kip authorized the formation of the local parish that became St. Stephen's. Dr. Hays was the founding Warden of that congregation.

The doctor's daughters and son Eric assisted him when he was elected the city's first Coroner. The father taught his children to tell time and to record in a ledger in their home the hour and minute they heard gunshots in the city. His children's entries came in handy when Coroner Hays needed to determine the time of death when called to testify at murder trials.

Prior to 1872, potable water for residents in the city of San Luis Obispo was supplied by horse-drawn water carts. In that year, Hays formed a partnership of entrepreneurs to delivery pure fresh water by aqueduct.

For two and a half years, Dr. Hays traveled to California hospitals and studied their floor designs, service protocols, and administration. Through his direction, the two storied San Luis Obispo County Hospital and Farm opened for patients on St. Valentine's Day 1879. In addition to Dr. Hays, the hospital staff was composed of a male nurse, a building and grounds manager, and a cook. The natural spring located on the hospital grounds provided water for the facility's operations and for the farm where indigent patients and their families could raise vegetables.

Dr. Hays served as Master of King David's Lodge from 1881 through 1884. In addition to being a Freemason, Hays was a member of the International Order of Odd Fellows, the Episcopal church, the National Guard, and the Grand Army of the Republic. The San Luis Obispo Medical Society was founded and chartered due to his promotion of the organization.

During his years in San Luis Obispo, Dr. Hays kept his interest in meteorology. He maintained detailed records of daily temperatures and rainfall. He copied this information into reports he sent to the Smithsonian Institution.

Hays Street, intersecting Grand Avenue north of Highway 101 in San Luis Obispo, is named for Dr. Hays.

THE MODERNIZATON

AND

THE RESTORATION

The 1970s were an interesting time in King David's history. If things had gone as expected, the Marsh Street Temple would now be a commercial building in private hands.

At the July 7, 1971, Stated Meeting, W. Bro. Blodgett moved and W. Bro. Wiech seconded a motion of "approval of the action of the Masonic Hall Association in taking the necessary steps to act in procurement of property suitable for the location of a lodge hall." The vote was nineteen Yes, seven No, and one Blank.

Bro. Casper Weir penned a letter to Master Baumberger objecting to turning the exclusive control of a decision on a new Lodge over to the Masonic Hall Association, citing the matter was only noticed in the Trestleboard as a topic of discussion, that the motion's wording had confused several brothers, and that the motion was raised at a July meeting when many brothers are on vacation and attendance was low. W. Bro. Baumberger issued a letter with counter arguments.

As accusations of machinations flew, attempts were made to get the Grand Master and District Inspector into the fray. The brothers wanting to sell believed the cost of retrofitting the building to "the demands of the state and local fire marshals" to be prohibitive. Others moved forward to finance the "rehabilitation of the temple."

A small battle ran on through 1972 into 1973. There was a stockholders meeting on March 14, 1972, and the dissention between senior brethren and the hall association became even more apparent, prompting the Master to state, "... the Board of Directors of the Association ... in my opinion has no authority to challenge the stockholders action. ... It is my opinion that the coordination and speedy movement towards the acquisition of property and erection of a new Masonic Temple can be more readily accomplished under one body." He established a committee to "Prepare or cause to be prepared the proper resolution to abolish the entity now known as 'The Masonic Hall Association'." In September of 1972, motions were proposed to abolish the Masonic Hall Association, and a committee was formed to "study the feasibility of acquiring all outstanding stock in the Masonic Hall Association."

At the March 7, 1973, Stated Meeting, "The Advisory Committee of King David's Lodge, in reviewing the recommendations made by the Grand Lodge Committee on Lodge Financing at a meeting in San Francisco on October 12, 1972, proposes the following considerations. Each consideration is made in the form of a separate motion in order that they be individually considered." W. Bro. Blodgett seconded each of the five motions.

Number 4 was the key motion, "It is moved that the Worshipful Master of King David's Lodge be instructed to present a Resolution to the membership authorizing the establishment of a Standing Committee for the purpose of over-seeing the reorganization of the Masonic Hall Association' the ultimate acquisition of a new building site if necessary' and the construction of a new Masonic Temple."

Master Eldon Nelson wrote a letter to all members stating in part, "There is no question that the present Temple will have to be replaced within the foreseeable future. ...For us to afford a new Temple it undoubtedly will have to be located out of the central business district. This would eliminate the possibility of tenant income. ...Whereas on October 15, 1972, the Grand Lodge Committee on Lodge Financing again reaffirmed their position and again encouraged an organized move toward the acquisition of a new temple ..."

At the November 7, 1973, Stated Meeting, a secret ballot was taken and by a two-thirds majority, the resolution of March 7th was reversed. By 1978, W. Bro. Wiech was President of the Masonic Hall Association and his letter of September 6, illustrated the changing tide on the issue of selling the Marsh Street building. *"As some of you may know, the Hall Association has retained an architect, to assist us in refurbishing our existing temple building. The chances of building a new temple in the near future are very dim, due to the cost of land, labor and financing money. The days of a one purpose building are gone and one has to have rentals in addition to our own masonic bodies, in order to survive."*

THE RENOVATIONS

The San Luis Obispo architect chosen to prepare the renovation blueprints in 1978 was Jonathan Lindenthaler.

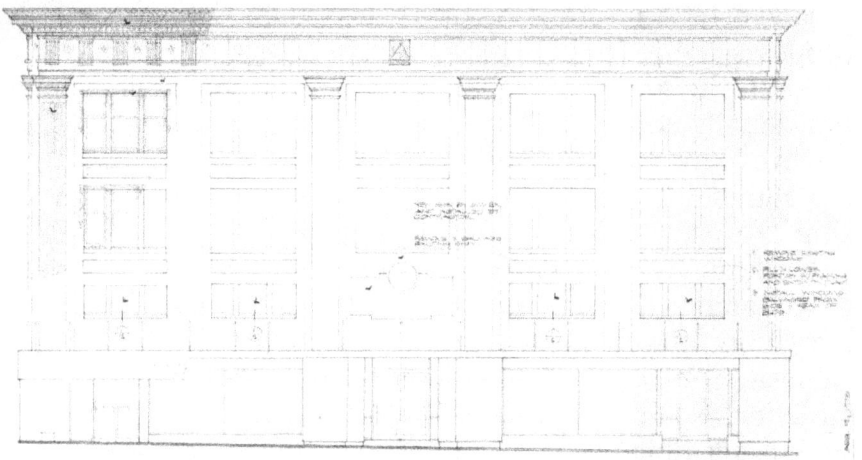

1978 New Front Elevation and Remodel

The renovations included $48,600 for removing and repairing to the outside rear wall; $547.73 to recover the lodge chairs; painting the second floor for $7,000 to $10,000; carpeting the stairways and second floor for $6,000; installing a new ventilation shaft to the boiler room; $3,000 to remodel the ladies lounge; $15,000 to upgrade the electrical wiring;

and $14,000 to modernize the kitchen. Along the way, the front entrance remodel was included and refinishing the dining room floor. At the June 6, 1979, Stated Meeting, discussion was had when the Masonic Hall Association said it could not afford to install an elevator, and Bro. Birkes moved to abolish the Hall Association; the motion failed.

By April 1, 1981, W. Bro. Bill Edwards was able to report on the progress and speed of construction on the elevator. The Masonic Hall Association still exists.

The elevator tower is visible in this aerial view at the upper right corner of Temple. The eight skylight structure in lower right is the "Doghouse" that protects the large oculus in the Lodge room. The flag pole is a disguised cell phone tower.

*View of the 1970s façade. The prominent
name of Laws Hobby Center on the
awning caused many locals to mistakenly
believe the Hobby Center owned the building.*

*A giant blue Square and Compass
pendant lamp below the skylight
fills the stairwell with light at night.*

THE 2010 RESTORATION

In 2010, the brethren of both King David's Lodge and the Masonic Hall Association decided to restore the Temple's front façade to its original 1913 form and remodel the Assembly Room. Stone framework was fabricated in the manner of Hatch's original façade and the front reopened so the original twin flame lights could be seen just above the period oak doors and beveled glass at the rear of the indented portico.

A black and white mosaic pavement with a center blazing star and ornamented with an indented tessellated border was laid in the Tiler's room. The exposed fire sprinkler pipes in the Assembly room were removed and hidden sprinklers were installed in crown molding. The ceiling having been thus reopened to its original form, was painted with sky and clouds to represent the "canopy of heaven". The projects were funded with income from rentals and investments.

The 2010 reconstruction of the 1913 façade.

An Anachronism

There was no automated sprinkler system in the original building. There were "cistern holes" where firefighters could lift a lid and insert a fire hose. Water flowed down ductwork and sprayed out of perforated pipes to suppress any fire. The flanged black pipe depicted in the photograph is in the building's foyer. In 1913, the pipe would have remained in the hole and only the circular brass cap plate would have been removed by the firefighters. With the installation of modern fire suppression in the 1970s and upgrades in 2010, this system is only of historical interest.

THE 2007 CONSOLIDATION
ESTERO LODGE NO. 719

On January 1, 2007, Estero Lodge No. 719 in Morro Bay, California, consolidated with King David's Lodge. The brothers of Estero Lodge brought more than their fraternal friendship to the city of San Luis Obispo. Today, the beautiful crystal chandeliers that grace the ceiling of King David's Dining Room are from the Estero Temple in Morro Bay.

The $628,641 netted from the sale of the Morro Bay building and property on Highway 41 was divided between the Order of Easter Star and King David's Lodge. The monies to King David's Lodge became the fountainhead of a perpetual college scholarship fund for high school seniors in both the cities of San Luis Obispo and Morro Bay.

THE FESTIVITIES

The brethren of King David's Lodge have an active history of sundry fraternal fun. After the dedication celebration in 1913, the Grand Lodge officers and Lodge brethren were entertained by a comedic German impressionist.

A 15 x 12 foot stage in the Dining Hall, sported blue velvet curtains during the early decades. The stage was the venue for "Barbershop Quartets", musical recitals, public speakers, and varied entertainers. Prior to the advent of disc-jockeys, after-dinner dances in the Temple Dining Hall featured live bands.

The accompanying photograph of the dancer in front of the Lodge Room "Forest of Lebanon" wallpaper is from the May 17, 1947, "Sweethearts Night" where the brothers, their ladies, and guests were entertained after dinner by a three couple troop of professional Hollywood ballroom dancers.

Baseball field trips have included fireworks nights at the SLO Blues in Sinsheimer Stadium and numerous outings to Dodger Stadium in Los Angeles. Lodge minutes reflect that a 1974 bus trip to a Dodger Double Header cost each brother the mere total of $13.00. There have been outings to Hearst Castle, theatrical productions, Cal Poly basketball games, Cal Poly football games, and party boat fishing out of Virg's Landing in Morro Bay. Brothers have represented King David's Lodge in the San Luis Obispo Literacy Council's Spelling Bee Contest.

The billiard table mentioned on page 27 is gone, but there are still the pocket pool table and poker table in the basement Recreation Room. The brothers, their ladies, and guests gather in the room to watch the annual NFL Super Bowl Game and movies on a BIG screen television from plush leather lounge chairs. Refreshments are chilled in a large cast-iron claw footed tub removed from the third floor showers.

Monthly "simple fare fun dinners", Constitutional Day barbecues in the park, Hawaiian shirt and dinner night, and Sweethearts and Widows Dinners are in addition to annual recognition dinners for Firefighters, Peace Officers, and high school scholarship recipients. New social events for 2013 included a "Family and Friends Potluck Karaoke Night".

King David's Lodge has participated in memorable and frequent outdoor ritual degree conferrals and district degree conferrals over its history. However, it is a rare privilege for a Masonic Lodge to confer a degree at the request of the Grand Lodge of a foreign jurisdiction. Nevertheless, this has occurred twice in the illustrious history of King David's Lodge.

On March 21, 1973, Past Grand Master of Free China George W. Chen was in attendance when the brethren of King David's conferred a courtesy Second Degree on Bro. Yong Y. Louis of Liberty Lodge No. 7 of Taiwan, China. Past Master Caspar Weir of King David's obligated Bro. Louis.

Bro. Damian Kachlakev, PhD, is a Professor of Civil and Structural Engineering at CalPoly State University. He was a Fellowcraft in Vedar Lodge No. 18 in his native Bulgaria. After exchanges between the Grand Secretary of the United Grand Lodge of Bulgaria and the Grand Secretary of California, dispensation was granted to confer the Third Degree of Masonry on Bro. Kachlakev by King David's Lodge. On December 11, 2012, King David's brethren gathered and Raised Bro. Kachlakev to the sublime degree of Master Mason.

Concordant Masonic bodies that have been associated with the brethren of King David's include:
- San Luis Chapter of Royal Arch Masons
- San Luis Obispo Council of Royal and Select Masons
- San Luis Obispo Commandery of Knights Templar
- High Twelve International
- Corona Chapter of Order of the Eastern Star
- Al Malaikah Shrine
- Santa Barbara Scottish Rite
- San Luis Obispo Shrine Club
- San Luis Obispo Scottish Rite Club
- Order of the White Shrine of Jerusalem
- Channel Coast Council of Allied Masonic Degrees
- Southern California Research Lodge
- Brian Boru Council of Knight Masons
- District Officers Association
- International Order of the Rainbow for Girls
- Job's Daughters International
- Order of DeMolay
- National Sojourners
- Fresno Priory of Knights of the York Cross of Honor
- CIYRA - Channel Islands York Rite Association

Circa 1943 ("cedars" wallpaper on west wall
of Lodge Room has since been painted over with gold)

Masons are taught to be "On the Square", but it has nothing to do with the regular monthly square dancing sponsored in years past in the Dining Room of King David's Temple. What are regularly squared are cornerstones, and King David's Lodge has been involved in laying many cornerstones over the years; from Cal Poly in 1903 to Laguna Junior High in 1970 to the Morro Bay Firehouse in 2012. In those 108 years, cornerstones have been laid for three schools, the County Courthouse, the San Luis Obispo Federal Building, and a library.

There is always a group of nobles and their ladies who will head to Los Angeles for the Shrine Circus and special events. Shriners and Masonic brothers gather each year and walk or ride on hay bales in the Pinedorado Parade in Cambria.

Participation in civic parades has always been a fun part of the Masonic fellowship. With the exception of degree rituals and monthly business meetings, Masonic events and dinners at King David's are open to family, friends, and the public.

San Luis Obispo Knights Templar are proud of their Christian heritage and invite friends, families, and the public to attend their annual Christmas and Easter Observances.

The Knights Templar of San Luis Obispo
Commandery No. 27 gathered for
their Easter Observance on April 12, 1914,
in front of the Marsh Street Temple

*San Luis Obispo Sir Knights participating
in a Long Beach 1921 parade*

The object in this photograph is indeed a children's "bounce house" erected in the center of the Temple's Lodge Room. The Cedars wallpaper is clearly visible in the background. The party event was courtesy of Bro. Christian Marano and his family.

In recent decades, the Lodge Room has been the scene of piano & brass jazz ensembles, a harpist recital, comical "stick pony" races for charity, "in the round" theatrical productions, Philippine youth ethnic dance exhibitions, historical lectures by a professor from the nearby California Polytechnic State University, slide presentations of foreign travels by members of the Lodge, "On the Level" public Masonic education, and several performances by professional magicians.

King David's Lodge offers both the spiritual growth found in the solemn rituals of Freemasonry, fraternal socializing, and frolicking with wives, family, friends, neighbors, and visitors, all to be experienced in the ambiance of our historic Temple.

THE CHARITY

AND

THE FUTURE

*Freemasonry is an order whose leading star
is philanthropy, and whose principles
inculcate an unceasing devotion
to the cause of virtue and morality*

Marquis de La Fayette

Masonic charity assumes many forms in San Luis Obispo. While King David's monetary donations are vast and numerous, there is much more brotherly relief on the fraternal level.

During both World Wars, many young men found themselves transferred away from their home Lodges and posted to San Luis Obispo or Morro Bay. During WWII, fifty-five such men had not yet completed their three degrees of Masonry at home. At the requests of the Grand Lodges for these out-of-state men, the brethren of King David's conferred the degrees.

During both World Wars, King David's Lodge purchased war bonds. Lodge blood donor drives started during WWI and were active again during WWII. After Korea, the brothers started regular blood donations at the Lodge. The donated blood went on an account with the blood bank that made units available for any brother or family member in need of transfusions.

For several decades, the brothers operated a fingerprint identification program at the County Fair for children, until the program was taken over by local law enforcement agencies. There is a monthly group of brothers that removes litter from of a section of local highway as part of the state beautification program. The brothers cook an annual barbecue for the children, staff, and families at Hawthorne Elementary School.

Brothers drive Masonic widows to appointments and assist them with legal paperwork and household or yard chores.

Education has always been a major consideration when directing Masonic philanthropic gifts. In 2012, King David's Lodge donated $17,500 in scholarships for local high school seniors, $2,500 to Discretionary Funds for Principals at local schools, $500 for Fireman Paramedic training, $5,000 for the Grand Master's Literacy project (2011 was $5,000 to train oncology nurses), and $1,000 to Cal Poly. In addition to the scholarships, King David's philanthropy includes gifts to Rainbow Girls, the Grand Master's Project, local schools, and additional general charitable gifts of $30,000 to $40,000.

Recent Lodge philanthropy has supported a broad spectrum of charitable groups, projects, and relief agencies, including: the Alisa Ann Ruch Fire Camp for children who are burn victims, the Maxine Lewis Homeless shelter, San Luis Obispo Hospice, the local literacy council, care packages for our overseas troops, the Boy Scouts' Camp French, Dr. Noor Foundation, Alzheimer research and support, the local Historical Society, the Masonic Homes, Campfire Girls, the rescue zoo in Paso Robles, the victims of 9-11, Habitat for Humanity, Multiple Sclerosis Society, Grizzly Youth Academy, SARP rape crisis support, American Heart Association, the victims of the earthquakes in Haiti and in Peru, the victims of hurricanes Katrina and Sandy, tornado victim relief, Breast Cancer Walk, Masonic Service Association Veterans Care, and local youth athletic and academic support programs.

The brethren of King David's Lodge have been active in San Luis Obispo for one hundred and forty-three years. The Marsh Street Temple has served as their home for one hundred years. As long as San Luis Obispo has men who value Brotherly Love, Relief, and Truth, then Faith, Hope, and Charity will radiate from our Masonic Temple. It is the ardent hope of the current brethren of King David's Lodge that, at the Bi-centennial of our beautiful Masonic facility in 2113, our future Masonic brothers will look back at us with the same appreciation we have for the remarkable brothers who established and built Freemasonry in San Luis Obispo over a century ago.

ABOUT THE AUTHOR

Peter George Champion has been a California attorney for over thirty-five years. His diverse background includes time in the South Pacific as a merchant seaman, a professional actor, an elementary school classroom teacher, a junior high school industrial arts instructor, manager of an Italian restaurant, and an operator of commercial apiaries.

He has been a Freemason since 1972 and has the privilege of serving as Worshipful Master of King David's Lodge in 2013. He is an officer in the San Luis Royal Arch Chapter No. 62, San Luis Obispo Cryptic Council No. 38, Knights Templar Commandery No. 27, and Channel Coast Council No. 114 of Allied Masonic Degrees. He is a member of several Masonic organizations in Southern California, including; Al Malaikah Shrine in Los Angeles, Brian Boru Council No. 38 Knight Masons in Long Beach, Southern California Research Lodge, and Santa Barbara Scottish Rite.

He is the author of the fun and entertaining book:
Masonic Trivia, Amusements & Curiosities

www.ingramcontent.com/pod-product-compliance
Lightning Source LLC
Chambersburg PA
CBHW070603290526
45790CB00002B/754